Parrots and Cheating Cheetahs

A Collection of Themed Poems

Heinemann
LIBRARY

www.heinemann.co.uk

Visit our website to find out more information about **Heinemann Library** books.

To order:
 Phone 44 (0) 1865 888066
 Send a fax to 44 (0) 1865 314091
 Visit the Heinemann Bookshop at www.heinemann.co.uk to browse our catalogue and order online.

First published in Great Britain by Heinemann Library, Halley Court, Jordan Hill, Oxford OX2 8EJ, a division of Reed Educational and Professional Publishing Ltd. Heinemann is a registered trademark of Reed Educational & Professional Publishing Limited.

OXFORD MELBOURNE AUCKLAND JOHANNESBURG BLANTYRE
GABORONE IBADAN PORTSMOUTH NH (USA) CHICAGO

© Reed Educational and Professional Publishing Ltd 2000
The moral right of the proprietor has been asserted.

Originated by Dot Gradations Ltd, Wickford
Printed in Hong Kong

04 03 02 01 00
10 9 8 7 6 5 4 3 2 1

ISBN 0 431 07512 3
This title is also available in a big book edition 0 431 07412 7

British Library Cataloguing in Publication Data
Parrots & Cheating Cheetahs: a collection of themed poems. – (Poetry Hour)
1. Children's poetry, English
I. Martin, Peggy-Lou
821'.008

The publishers gratefully acknowledge the following for permission to reproduce copyright material. Every effort has been made to trace copyright holders, but in some cases have proved impossible. The publishers would be happy to hear from any copyright holder that has not been acknowledged.

Acknowledgements
Alan Marks, pp4-5; David Holmes, pp6-7; Diana Mayo, pp16-17, 28-29, 30-31; Susan Winter, pp10-11; Rhiannon Powell, pp12-13; Dom Mansell, pp14-15; Valerie McBride, p16; Tom Kenyon, p18; Allan Curless, p20; Lisa Smith, p21; Mick Reid, pp22-23, 24-25; Jocelyn Wild, pp26-27.

Green Song by Judith Nicholls. © Judith Nicholls 1988, reprinted by permission of the author; **The Baby of the Family** by Wendy Cope, from 'Casting A Spell' published by Orchard Books © Wendy Cope. Reprinted by permission of the author; **The Court Jester's Last Report to the King** by Jack Prelutsky. Copyright untraced; **Supply Teacher** by Allan Ahlberg, from 'Please Mrs Butler' by Allan Ahlberg (Kestrel 1983) (pg 16, 16 lines) Copyright © Allan Ahlberg 1983. Reprinted by permission of Penguin Books Limited; **The Cheetah, My Dearest, Is Known Not to Cheat** by George Baker, from 'Runes and Tunes and Chimes' published by Faber and Faber Limited. Reprinted by permission of the publisher; **A Cast of Hawks** from 'A Bundle of Beasts' by Patricia Hooper. Text copyright © 1987 by Patricia Hooper. Reprinted by permission of Houghton Mifflin Company. All rights reserved; **Cat** by Eleanor Farjeon, from 'Silver Sand and Snow', published by Michael Joseph. Reprinted by permission of David Higham Associates Limited; **Roger the Dog** by Ted Hughes from 'What If The Truth?' by Ted Hughes published by Faber and Faber Limited. Reprinted by permission of the publisher; **Grim and Gloomy** from 'The Complete Poems for Children' by James Reeves, published by Heinemann. Reprinted by permission of Laura Cecil Literary Agency on behalf of the James Reeves Estate.

Poetry Hour is a version of selected poems from Heinemann Primary's Poetry Parade.

Contents

Windy Nights

by Robert Louis Stevenson

Whenever the moon and stars are set,
  Whenever the wind is high,
All night long in the dark and wet,
  A man goes riding by.
Late in the night when the fires are out,
Why does he gallop and gallop about?

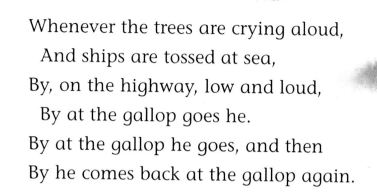

Whenever the trees are crying aloud,
  And ships are tossed at sea,
By, on the highway, low and loud,
  By at the gallop goes he.
By at the gallop he goes, and then
By he comes back at the gallop again.

What is Pink?

by Christina Rossetti

What is pink? a rose is pink
By the fountain's brink.
What is red? a poppy's red
In its barley bed.
What is blue? the sky is blue
Where the clouds float through.
What is white? a swan is white
Sailing in the light.
What is yellow? pears are yellow,
Rich and ripe and mellow.
What is green? the grass is green,
With small flowers between.
What is violet? clouds are violet
In the summer twilight.
What is orange? why, an orange,
Just an orange!

Green Song

by Judith Nicholls

Trees are green
and peas are green
but what's the very
greenest green?

A runner bean
and knees are green
when rolling in the grass
they've been.

A caterpillar's
nose is green,
seaweed between
your toes is green.

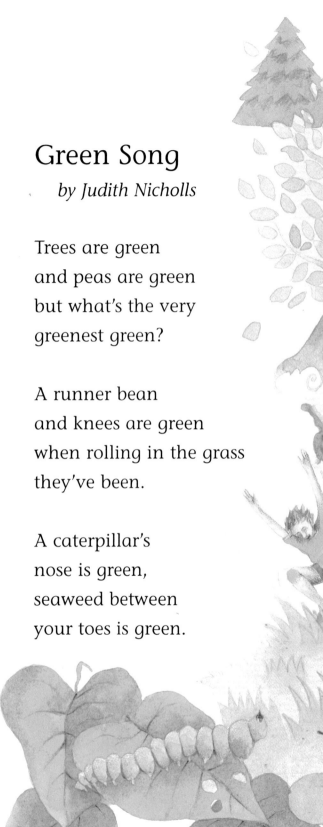

A frog beneath
his log is green,
a thick pea-soupy
fog is green.

A nettle's green,
an apple's green,
a mouldy cheese
is old and green
but what's the very
greenest green
of all the greens
that you have seen?

9

The Baby of the Family

by Wendy Cope

Up on Daddy's shoulders
He is riding high –
The baby of the family,
A pleased, pork pie.
I'm tired and my feet are sore –
It seems all wrong.
He's lucky to be little
But it won't last long.

The baby of the family,
He grabs my toys
And when I grab them back he makes
A big, loud noise.
I mustn't hit him, so I chant
This short, sweet song:
"You're lucky to be little
But it won't last long."

Everybody looks at him
and thinks he's sweet,
Even when he bellows "No!"
And stamps his feet.
He won't be so amusing
When he's tall and strong.
It's lovely being little
But it won't last long.

11

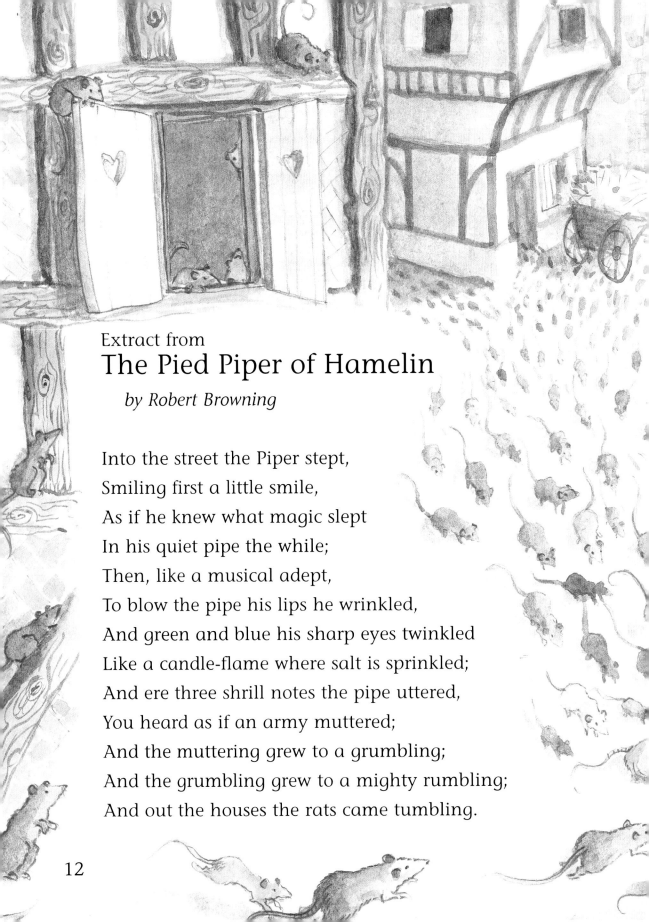

Extract from
The Pied Piper of Hamelin

by Robert Browning

Into the street the Piper stept,
Smiling first a little smile,
As if he knew what magic slept
In his quiet pipe the while;
Then, like a musical adept,
To blow the pipe his lips he wrinkled,
And green and blue his sharp eyes twinkled
Like a candle-flame where salt is sprinkled;
And ere three shrill notes the pipe uttered,
You heard as if an army muttered;
And the muttering grew to a grumbling;
And the grumbling grew to a mighty rumbling;
And out the houses the rats came tumbling.

Great rats, small rats, lean rats, brawny rats,
Brown rats, black rats, grey rats, tawny rats,
Grave old plodders, gay young friskers,
Fathers, mothers, uncles, cousins,
Cocking tails and pricking whiskers,
Families by tens and dozens,
Brothers, sisters, husbands, wives –
Followed the Piper for their lives.

The Court Jester's Last Report to the King

by Jack Prelutsky

Oh sire! My sire! your castle's on fire,
I fear it's about to explode,
a hideous lizard has eaten the wizard,
the prince has turned into a toad.

Oh sire! Good sire! there's woe in the shire,
fierce trolls are arriving in force,
there are pirates in port, monstrous ogres at court,
and a dragon has melted your horse.

Oh sire! Great sire! the tidings are dire,
a giant has trampled the school,
your army has fled, there are bees in your bed
and your nose has come off......APRIL FOOL!

The Table and the Chair

by Edward Lear

Said the Table to the Chair,
"You can hardly be aware
How I suffer from the heat,
And from chilblains on my feet!
If we took a little walk,
We might have a little talk!
Pray let us take the air!"
Said the Table to the Chair.

Said the Chair unto the Table,
"Now you *know* we are not able!"
How foolishly you talk,
When you know we *cannot* walk!"
Said the Table with a sigh,
"It can do no harm to try;
I've as many legs as you,
Why can't we walk on two?"

So they both went slowly down,
And walked about the town
With a cheerful bumpy sound,
As they toddled round and round.
And everybody cried,
As they hastened to their side,
"See! the Table and the Chair
Have come out to take the air!"

But in going down an alley,
To a castle in the valley,
They completely lost their way,
And wandered all the day,
Till, to see them safely back,
They paid a Ducky-quack,
And a Beetle and a Mouse,
Who took them to their house.

Then they whispered to each other,
"O delightful little brother!
What a lovely walk we've taken!
Let us dine on Beans and Bacon!"
So the Ducky and the leetle
Browny-Mousy and the Beetle
Dined, and danced upon their heads
Till they toddled to their beds.

Who Are You?

by Emily Dickinson

I'm Nobody! Who are you?
Are you – Nobody – too?
Then there's a pair of us?
Don't tell! they'd advertise – you know!

How dreary – to be – Somebody!
How public – like a Frog –
To tell one's name – the livelong June –
To an admiring Bog!

Supply Teacher

by Allan Ahlberg

Here is a rule for what to do
Whenever your teacher has the flu,
Or for some other reason takes to her bed
And a different teacher comes instead.

When this visiting teacher hangs up her hat,
Writes the date on the board, does this or that;
Always remember, you must say this:
"*Our* teacher never does that, Miss!"

When you want to change places or wander about,
Or feel like getting the guinea-pig out,
Never forget, the message is this:
"*Our* teacher always lets us, Miss!"

Then, when your teacher returns next day
And complains about the paint or clay,
Remember these words, you just say this:
"That *other* teacher told us to, Miss!"

Extract from
The Mad Gardener's Song

by Lewis Carroll

He thought he saw a Buffalo
  Upon the chimney-piece:
He looked again, and found it was
  His Sister's Husband's Niece
"Unless you leave this house," he said,
  "I'll send for the Police!"

He thought he saw a Banker's Clerk
  Descending from the bus:
He looked again, and found it was
  A Hippopotamus:
"If this should stay to dine," he said,
  "There won't be much for us!"

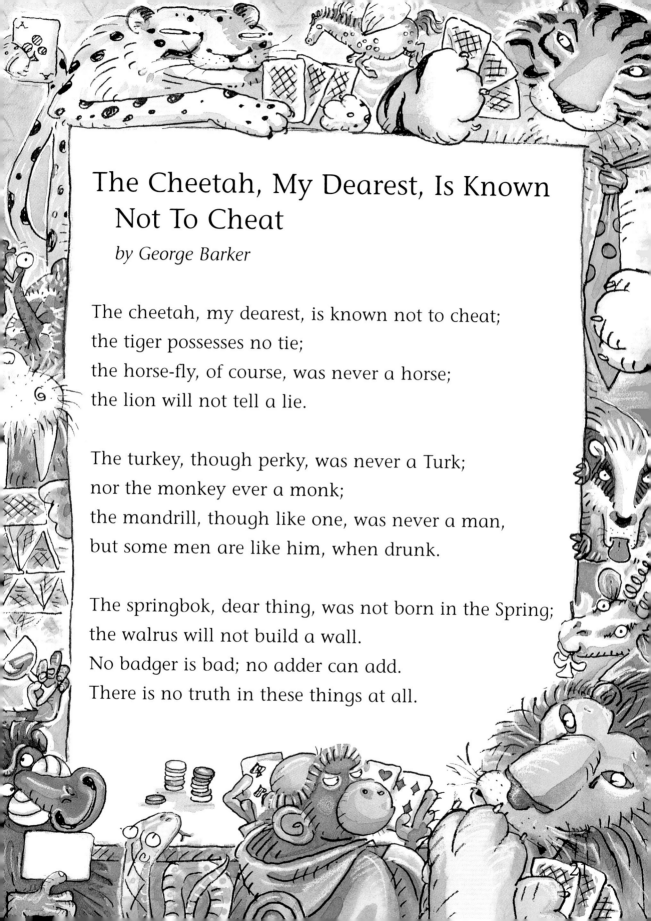

The Cheetah, My Dearest, Is Known Not To Cheat

by George Barker

The cheetah, my dearest, is known not to cheat;
the tiger possesses no tie;
the horse-fly, of course, was never a horse;
the lion will not tell a lie.

The turkey, though perky, was never a Turk;
nor the monkey ever a monk;
the mandrill, though like one, was never a man,
but some men are like him, when drunk.

The springbok, dear thing, was not born in the Spring;
the walrus will not build a wall.
No badger is bad; no adder can add.
There is no truth in these things at all.

A Cast of Hawks

by Patricia Hooper

"Come and sit," said the hawks.
"We are giving a play."

"In your house?" asked the mouse.
"But I really can't stay."

"In your lair?" asked the hare.
"But it's getting quite late."

"In your den?" asked the wren.
"But I see you've a plate!"

"Come and see," said the hawks.
"We are giving a show."

"Just for us?" asked the mouse.
"Well, perhaps. Maybe so."

"I'll be there," said the hare.
"But I wish you were storks."

"Don't go in," cried the wren,
"For I see they have forks!"

"Please applaud," said the hawks,
"And we'll start to perform."

"Our applause," said the mouse,
"Couldn't do any harm."

"Do we dare?" asked the hare.
"Then the play shall begin!"

"Must the actors wear bibs?
We must run!" cried the wren.

Cat

by Eleanor Farjeon

Cat!
Scat!
After her, after her,
Sleeky flatterer,
Spitfire chatterer,
Scatter her, scatter her
    Off her mat!
    Wuff!
    Wuff!
    Treat her rough!

Git her, git her,
Whiskery spitter!
Catch her, catch her,
Green-eyed scratcher!
    Slathery
    Slithery
    Hisser,
    Don't miss her!

Run till you're dithery,
  Hithery
  Thithery
  Pfitts! Pfitts!
  How she spits!
  Spitch! Spatch!
  Can't she scratch!

Scritching the bark
Of the sycamore-tree,
She's reached her ark
And's hissing at me
      Pfitts! Pfitts!
      Wuff! Wuff!

Scat,
Cat!
That's
That!

25

Roger the Dog

by Ted Hughes

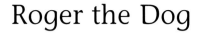

Asleep he wheezes at his ease.
He only wakes to scratch his fleas.

He hogs the fire, he bakes his head
As if it were a loaf of bread.

He's just a sack of snoring dog.
You can lug him like a log.

You can roll him with your foot.
He'll stay snoring where he's put.

Take him out for exercise
He'll roll in cowclap up to his eyes.

He will not race, he will not romp.
He saves his strength for gobble and chomp.

He'll work as hard as you could wish
Emptying the dinner dish.

Then flops flat, and digs down deep,
Like a miner, into sleep.

Grim and Gloomy

by James Reeves

Oh, grim and gloomy,
So grim and gloomy
Are the caves beneath the sea.
Oh, rare but roomy
And bare and boomy,
Those salt sea caverns be.

Oh, slim and slimy
Or grey and grimy
Are the animals of the sea.
Salt and oozy
And safe and snoozy
The caves where those animals be.

Hark to the shuffling,
Huge and snuffling,
Ravenous, cavernous, great sea-beasts!
But fair and fabulous,
Tintinnabulous,
Gay and fabulous are their feasts.

Ah, but the queen of the sea,
The querulous, perilous sea!
How the curls of her tresses
The pearls on her dresses,
Sway and swirl in the waves,
How cosy and dozy,
How sweet ring a-rosy
Her bower in the deep-sea caves!

Oh, rare but roomy
And bare and boomy
Those caverns under the sea,
And grave and grandiose
Safe and sandiose
The dens of her denizens be.

Mother Parrot's Advice to her Children

a poem from Ganda, Africa, translated by A. K. Nyabongo

Never get up till the sun gets up,
Or the mists will give you a cold,
And a parrot whose lungs have once been touched
Will never live to be old.

Never eat plums that are not quite ripe,
For perhaps they will give you a pain;
And never dispute what the hornbill says,
Or you'll never dispute again.

Never despise the power of speech;
Learn every word as it comes,
For this is the pride of the parrot race,
That it speaks in a thousand tongues.

Never stay up when the sun goes down,
But sleep in your own home bed,
And if you've been good, as a parrot should,
You will dream that your tail is red.

Index of first lines